POP HITS

Unique, Distinctive Piano Arrangements of 20 Hit Songs

ISBN 978-1-4950-0234-2

HAL•LEONARD®
CORPORATION

7777 W. BLUEMOUND RD. P.O. BOX 13819 MILWAUKEE, WI 53213

Visit Hal Leonard Online at
www.halleonard.com

CONTENTS

BEAUTIFUL DAY

Words by BONO
Music by U2

8

BILLIE JEAN

Words and Music by
MICHAEL JACKSON

To Coda

12

D.S. al Coda
(with repeat)

CODA

13

BOULEVARD OF BROKEN DREAMS

Words by BILLIE JOE
Music by GREEN DAY

BREAKEVEN

Words and Music by STEPHEN KIPNER,
ANDREW FRAMPTON, DANIEL O'DONOGHUE
and MARK SHEEHAN

FIELDS OF GOLD

Music and Lyrics by
STING

23

GET LUCKY

Words and Music by THOMAS BANGALTER,
GUY MANUEL HOMEM CHRISTO,
PHARRELL WILLIAMS and NILE RODGERS

Andante, in the style of George Winston

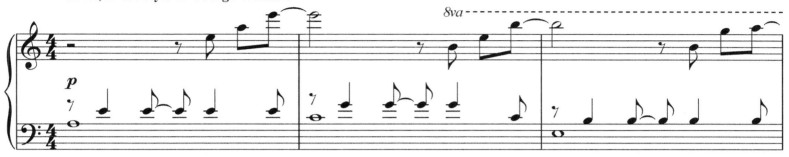

*play cue notes
second time only*

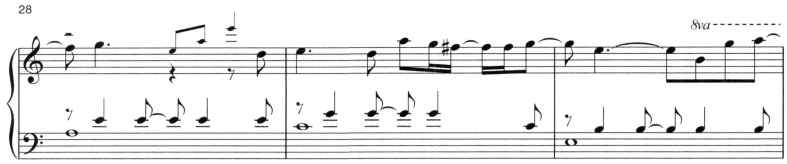

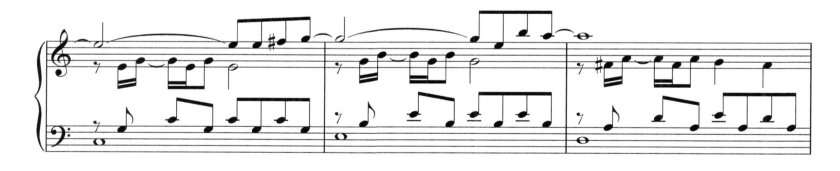

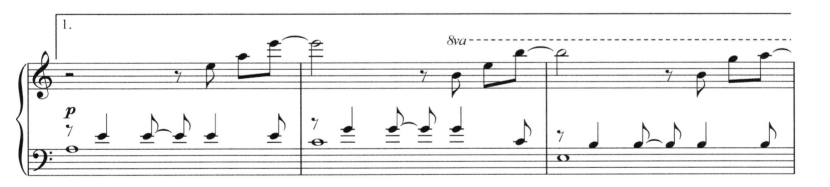

HAPPY
from DESPICABLE ME 2

Words and Music by
PHARRELL WILLIAMS

Moderately fast Blues

To Coda

HO HEY

Words and Music by JEREMY FRAITES
and WESLEY SCHULTZ

40

JUST THE WAY YOU ARE

Words and Music by BRUNO MARS, ARI LEVINE,
PHILIP LAWRENCE, KHARI CAIN
and KHALIL WALTON

Light Latin Jazz groove

I'M YOURS

Words and Music by
JASON MRAZ

Leisurely, flowing freely

LET IT GO
from Disney's Animated Feature FROZEN

Music and Lyrics by KRISTEN ANDERSON-LOPEZ
and ROBERT LOPEZ

Half-time feel, mysterious

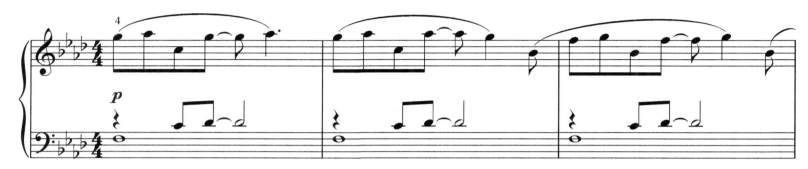

With pedal

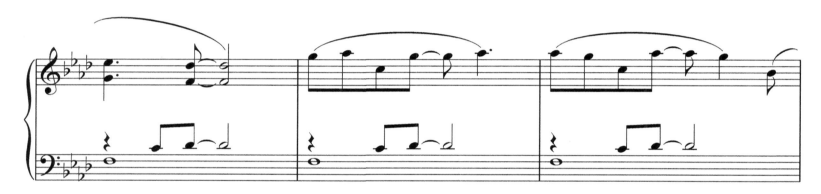

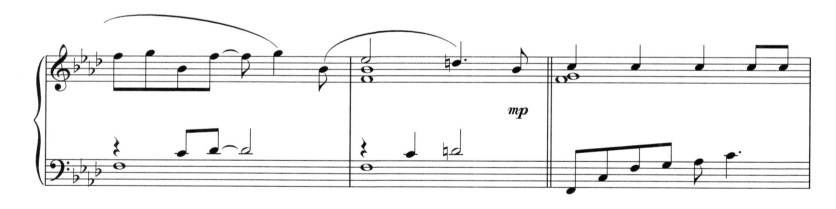

To Coda

ROLLING IN THE DEEP

Words and Music by ADELE ADKINS
and PAUL EPWORTH

Moderate McCoy Tyner vibe

POKER FACE

Words and Music by STEFANI GERMANOTTA
and RedOne

Bright Funk

66

RADIOACTIVE

Words and Music by DANIEL REYNOLDS,
BENJAMIN McKEE, DANIEL SERMON,
ALEXANDER GRANT and JOSH MOSSER

Flowing, not too fast

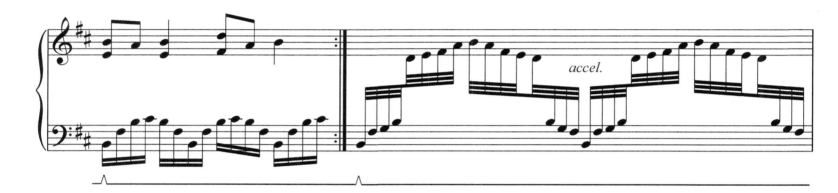

Steady Ballad tempo

ROAR

Words and Music by KATY PERRY, LUKASZ GOTTWALD,
MAX MARTIN, BONNIE McKEE
and HENRY WALTER

ROYALS

Words and Music by ELLA YELICH-O'CONNOR
and JOEL LITTLE

Moderately, in a Baroque style

D.S. al Coda

CODA

mf

molto rit.

SMELLS LIKE TEEN SPIRIT

Words and Music by KURT COBAIN,
KRIST NOVOSELIC and DAVE GROHL

Moderately, like a New Age Ballad

cresc.

To Coda ⊕

mf

84

D.S. al Coda

CODA

STRONGER
(What Doesn't Kill You)

Words and Music by GREG KURSTIN,
JORGEN ELOFSSON, DAVID GAMSON
and ALEXANDRA TAMPOSI

To Coda ⊕

D.S. al Coda

CODA

VIVA LA VIDA

Words and Music by GUY BERRYMAN,
JON BUCKLAND, WILL CHAMPION
and CHRIS MARTIN

To Coda ⊕

CODA

WONDERWALL

Words and Music by
NOEL GALLAGHER

Play 4 times

molto rit.

YOUR FAVORITE MUSIC
ARRANGED FOR PIANO SOLO

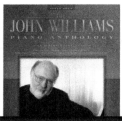

ARTIST, COMPOSER, TV & MOVIE SONGBOOKS

**Adele for Piano Solo –
3rd Edition**
00820186..................................$19.99

The Beatles Piano Solo
00294023..................................$17.99

**A Charlie Brown
Christmas**
00313176..................................$17.99

**Paul Cardall –
The Hymns Collection**
00295925..................................$24.99

Coldplay for Piano Solo
00307637..................................$17.99

**Selections from
Final Fantasy**
00148699..................................$19.99

**Alexis Ffrench – The
Sheet Music Collection**
00345258..................................$19.99

Game of Thrones
00199166..................................$19.99

Hamilton
00354612..................................$19.99

**Hillsong Worship
Favorites**
00303164..................................$14.99

How to Train Your Dragon
00138210..................................$22.99

Elton John Collection
00306040..................................$24.99

La La Land
00283691..................................$14.99

John Legend Collection
00233195..................................$17.99

Les Misérables
00290271..................................$19.99

Little Women
00338470..................................$19.99

Outlander: The Series
00254460..................................$19.99

**The Peanuts®
Illustrated Songbook**
00313178..................................$29.99

**Astor Piazzolla –
Piano Collection**
00285510..................................$19.99

**Pirates of the Caribbean –
Curse of the Black Pearl**
00313256..................................$19.99

Pride & Prejudice
00123854..................................$17.99

Queen
00289784..................................$19.99

John Williams Anthology
00194555..................................$24.99

George Winston Piano Solos
00306822..................................$22.99

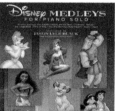

MIXED COLLECTIONS

**Beautiful Piano
Instrumentals**
00149926..................................$16.99

**Best Jazz
Piano Solos Ever**
00312079..................................$24.99

Best Piano Solos Ever
00242928..................................$22.99

**Big Book of
Classical Music**
00310508..................................$24.99

Big Book of Ragtime Piano
00311749..................................$22.99

Christmas Medleys
00350572..................................$16.99

Disney Medleys
00242588..................................$19.99

Disney Piano Solos
00313128..................................$17.99

Favorite Pop Piano Solos
00312523..................................$16.99

Great Piano Solos
00311273..................................$19.99

**The Greatest Video
Game Music**
00201767..................................$19.99

Most Relaxing Songs
00233879..................................$17.99

**Movie Themes
Budget Book**
00289137..................................$14.99

**100 of the Most Beautiful
Piano Solos Ever**
00102787..................................$29.99

100 Movie Songs
00102804..................................$29.99

Peaceful Piano Solos
00286009..................................$17.99

**Piano Solos for
All Occasions**
00310964..................................$24.99

**River Flows in You &
Other Eloquent Songs**
00123854..................................$17.99

Sunday Solos for Piano
00311272..................................$17.99

Top Hits for Piano Solo
00294635..................................$14.99

View songlists online and order from your
favorite music retailer at
halleonard.com

*Prices, content, and availability subject
to change without notice.*

Disney characters and artwork TM & © 2021 Disney

0722
195